THE
Great Depression

by
Walter A. Hazen

Cover Graphics by
Vickie Lane

Cover Photo
Corbis-Bettmann

Publisher
Instructional Fair • TS Denison
Grand Rapids, Michigan 49544

Permission to Reproduce

About the Author

Walter A. Hazen received his Bachelor of Science in Education from Troy State University. He also holds a master's degree from the University of Tennessee, where he specialized in deaf education. A secondary history teacher with over 30 years of experience, Walter spent the last several years of his career teaching and developing curriculum for deaf students.

Credits

Author: Walter A. Hazen
Cover Graphics: Vickie Lane
Project Director/Editor: Sharon Kirkwood
Editors: Lisa Hancock, Linda Triemstra
Production/Layout: Pat Geasler, Vickie Lane

Photos   Corbis–Bettmann
          UPI/Corbis–Bettmann

Standard Book Number: 1-56822-628-4
The Great Depression
Copyright © 1998 by Instructional Fair • TS Denison
2400 Turner Avenue NW
Grand Rapids, Michigan 49544

Table of Contents

Introduction 4

The Party Before the Storm 5–6

Black Thursday, Blacker Tuesday 7

Spending and Speculation 8–9

Bread Lines and Soup Kitchens 10–11

Apples for Sale 12

A Cardboard Roof 13

The Plight of the Farmer.. 14

A Bold Request and a Federal Fiasco 15–16

A New President, a New Hope 17

The Hundred Days 18

Soldiers of the Soil 19–20

The National Recovery Administration 21–22

Dust and Desperation 23–24

Safety Down the Road 25

Radio, Puzzles, and Other Pastimes 26

Public Enemies, Private Heroes 27

People of Color Suffer Injustice............................ 28–29

Popularity, Resistance, and Roosevelt's Second Term 30

A Decade of Endings and Beginnings 31

Answer Key/Selected Bibliography 32

Depressions, or panics as they are often called in textbooks, have occurred throughout America's history. The first began in 1785 and the last in 1929. In between there were severe depressions in 1837, 1873, 1893, and 1907. Each lasted several years and took its toll on the nation. But none can compare with the Great Depression of 1929 in length and severity.

The Great Depression stands as the worst economic disaster in U.S. history. Lasting for over a decade, it affected every type of business and industry. At its height, unemployment rose to nearly 13 million, and America became a nation of bread lines and soup kitchens. Only massive federal programs initiated by President Roosevelt's New Deal prevented the depression from becoming worse. Even then, the economy did not fully recover until the start of World War II.

This book surveys the factors that brought on this terrible period in history. It also addresses the steps taken to pull the nation out of its economic doldrums. But the main focus of the book is on people: how they survived those trying years; how they put food in their stomachs; what they thought; how they behaved; and, finally, how they maintained their sanity in the midst of a world that was fast crumbling around them.

Few events in history have had a more profound effect on the American people than the Great Depression. Those who lived through it were never quite the same.

The Eye on History series strives to bring history to life through the personal experiences of those who lived them. The letters, diary accounts, postcards, and so on are fictitious. However, the facts contained in them represent what individuals might have written. The more students are able to experience history through what others may have felt and thought, the more meaningful it will be. After all, history is not just musty dates and facts. History is the stories of individuals and nations and of heroes and ordinary people. It is influenced by fashions and passions. We hope this series will help students understand history in new and exciting ways.

New York City
November 27, 1923

Dear Blanche,

I have been in New York for one month now, and life gets more exciting everyday. What a difference from Mobile, Alabama! What with goofy flagpole sitters and dance marathons, something crazy seems to be going on all the time.

Speaking of dance marathons, I watched one several nights ago for the first time. Well, I watched part of a dance marathon. I'm told these things can go on for several days. Couples dance like crazy until they can't stand, taking only brief breaks from time to time. Although they compete for prizes, I'm sure the challenge of outlasting all the other couples on the floor is what really motivates them. Say—did you read about that poor guy in Tonawanda (New York) who dropped dead on the dance floor? Really! I hear he had danced for more than 80 hours!

Well, I need to close. Five A.M. comes awfully early for the working girl. Say 'hello' to Bobby and Norma for me. I'll see you during your Christmas break.

Dottie

A devastating depression was the last thing on the minds of most Americans in the 1920s. Business was booming and times were good. The country was prospering and no one could envision the tremendous collapse that loomed over the horizon.

The 1920s in America are known by many names. To most people, they are the Roaring Twenties. To others they are the Jazz Age or the Era of Wonderful Nonsense. Still others refer to them as the Golden Age or the Lawless Decade. By whatever name they are called, the 1920s were, except to the poor, years of gaiety and excitement.

What brought on this unique period in American history that was also characterized by speculation in stock and by various get-rich schemes?

For the most part, it was the result of industrial expansion that took place during the First World War. Except for a brief depression that occurred as post-war America adjusted to a peacetime economy, the expansion resumed and resulted in an economic boom that brought prosperity to most Americans. Lower production costs made it possible for people to buy such things as automobiles and refrigerators, hitherto affordable only by the wealthy. Many Americans could also take vacations, go to the movies, and indulge in ball games and other sporting activities. Consumers were encouraged to spend, and chain stores and installment buying made it easy for them to comply. Many even had enough money to invest in the stock market and in real estate ventures.

Continued on page 6.

Continued from page 5.

The economic boom of the 1920s resulted in tremendous social changes. Innovations like canned goods and electric appliances helped liberate women from the home, and many took jobs for the first time. Some of the younger among them bobbed their hair, wore short skirts, and threw caution to the wind. Dubbed "flappers" by the press, these women smoked cigarettes, drank cocktails, wore lipstick, and danced a new dance called the Charleston. Young people in general revolted against the pre-World War I standards established by their parents and plunged headlong into the pursuit of thrills and excitement. Partying, dance marathons, and performing deeds of derring-do seemed foremost in their minds.

The 1920s was also an age of lawlessness. It was the era of the gangster and the bootlegger, brought on in large part by the passage of the 18th Amendment in 1919. The 18th Amendment prohibited the manufacture and sale of all alcoholic beverages in the United States. Its ratification was a boost for organized crime, which illegally manufactured beer and hard liquor and sold it in secret clubs called "speakeasies." Gang-type murders were frequent during the time, as rival gangs competed for control of the lucrative business.

Gangsterism aside, the 1920s for most Americans were happy and exciting years. People enjoyed themselves and got over the horrors of World War I. Because they thought the good times would go on forever, Americans were totally unprepared when their way of life changed so abruptly in October of 1929.

Discuss...

- what problems arise when consumers are encouraged to spend beyond their means.
- why moral standards underwent such radical changes in the years following World War I.
- how the behavior of young people today compares with their counterparts of the 1920s.
- how the 18th Amendment to the Constitution caused more problems than it solved.

Radio Report

New York City

November 1929

Rumors of investors jumping in droves from the windows of tall buildings on Wall Street have proven to be a myth. Some suicides have occurred, but nothing of the magnitude invented by the foreign press. It seems that a few of these tabloids would have the world believe that New Yorkers walking along sidewalks must literally step over the dead bodies of fallen brokers. That simply is not true.

New York police became quite concerned, however, when the market crashed on October 24 and rumors began to spread that 11 leading brokers had jumped to their deaths on Wall Street. While police headquarters was kept busy dispatching officers to confirm or disprove such reports, at least one humorous incident arose that showed just how frantic the situation had become.

On the afternoon alluded to, several police officers came upon a man standing on a ledge outside a window on the upper floor of a Wall Street building. One cautious officer approached the window and pleaded with the man not to jump. He assured the poor fellow that things were not as bad as they seemed; that life was indeed worth living.

"Who's jumping?" retorted the man on the ledge. "I'm just washing windows!"

The magnificent bubble of the 1920s burst on October 24, 1929. It was not a sudden occurrence, for the stock market had been fluctuating for months. But on that date, known as Black Thursday, almost 13 million shares changed hands on the New York Stock Exchange. A sudden panic had caused people to sell at whatever price they could get for their holdings. A total economic collapse was prevented when the nation's five leading bankers bought thousands of shares in various companies and temporarily shored up the market.

But the recovery was short-lived. Five days later, on October 29, investors once again panicked and more than 16 million shares were put up for sale on the New York exchange. Prices dropped sharply and many shares were soon found to be worthless. Americans who had speculated on the stock exchange soon discovered they had lost everything. Many had spent their life savings or borrowed money to buy stock, and now that stock was worthless. Those who suddenly found themselves left with nothing were not limited to the big brokers and investors. Quite the contrary. Everyone from housewives to waiters and taxi drivers had invested in the market. They too quickly realized they had lost everything.

The crash that occurred in October 1929 eventually affected all Americans and caused the worst depression in our nation's history. Factories and businesses closed, and unemployment soared. The depression spread worldwide and wrecked the economies of other nations. It lasted more than ten years and did not really end until the beginning of World War II, when the demand for war materials revitalized industry and put people back to work.

Discuss...

- the advantages and disadvantages of investing in stocks.
- how the collapse of the stock market could lead to widespread unemployment.
- whether you would ever borrow money or use savings to buy stock.
- how higher interest rates help curb spending and overspeculation.

March 12, 1930

Dear Mom and Dad,

I haven't written in some time because I didn't want to burden you with my problems. But matters have reached the point at which Dan and I may need to ask for your help.

Things seem to get worse everyday. First, the appliance store took away our refrigerator. Then that new furniture we bought on time last year was repossessed. I don't blame the men who carried it off last week; they were just doing their job. But it really hurt to see our beautiful sofa and chairs walking out the front door.

After we lost a bundle in the stock market and Dan was laid off at the mill, we needed money desperately. The first thing to go was the '28 Plymouth. I loved that car, and it broke my heart to watch some scoundrel drive it away for almost nothing. Dan had placed a sign on the windshield telling someone to make an offer, and we jumped at the $75. After all, we have two kids to feed.

You and Dad are lucky in some ways. You own your home and other things, and you never got trapped into this installment-buying thing. Who would have thought a depression could totally wipe out everything a person has?

My worst fear is that the bank will foreclose on the mortgage. If that happens, I don't know what we'll do. I guess we'll find ourselves out in the street.

I'll write more later. As I said, we may need a little help in the months ahead. I'll keep you posted.

Love,
Louise

The crash of the stock market was closely related to an overexpansion of credit. People not only borrowed money to buy stock but also began to purchase expensive items on the installment plan. Although installment buying on a small scale dates back to ancient times, it did not come into wide use until after World War I. Consumers availed themselves of this new innovation by buying furniture, appliances, automobiles, houses, and other necessities on credit. A little down, a little each month. No problem. It was so easy—until the bottom fell out of the economy in 1929. People lost their jobs and could no longer make the payments on the items they had purchased. Almost overnight, they lost everything. Installment buying declined, adding further to the depression.

Americans had also overspeculated in real estate in the years before the depression. Many who sought to get rich quickly borrowed money or used their savings to invest in the "Florida bubble." Land promoters convinced these unwary speculators that Florida was the place to amass a quick fortune by buying land cheaply and later selling it at a handsome profit. Even worthless

Continued on page 9.

Continued from page 8.

land could be sold at two or three times the amount paid for it because Florida—so it was advertised—was destined to become a year-round playground for the wealthy and a haven for citizens tired of the much colder climate of the North. And what worthless land much of it was! Some buyers who bought at a distance later discovered that their lots consisted of nothing but swamps and mangroves. Others purchased land miles from any settlement in areas where basics such as electricity and running water would not become commonplace until years later. To add to the problem, two severe hurricanes in 1926 made Florida less attractive in the eyes of some would-be land purchasers. In short, the Florida bubble burst, and many Americans who had subscribed to get-rich schemes lost everything they had.

The failure of banks was another cause of the depression. Americans had borrowed huge sums of money during the good years of the 1920s. When they lost their jobs and were unable to repay their loans, banks lost their sources of funds and had to close. In 1929, 642 banks failed. This number increased to 1,345 in 1930 and 2,298 in 1931. Americans with deposits in these banks were unable to reclaim their money. Many lost their life savings.

Finally, the failure of the federal government to act immediately after the stock market crashed heightened the effect of the depression. President Herbert Hoover believed the slump would be short-lived and chose not to interfere in the economy. He also believed that the hungry and the unemployed should receive aid at the local and state levels. By the time he realized that strong action on the part of the federal government was needed, the depression had worsened.

Discuss...
- which types of investments you consider the most secure (stocks, certificates of deposits, mutual funds, etc.)
- whether greater action on the part of President Hoover could have prevented the Great Depression.

For Debate
Resolved: That the disadvantages of buying on the installment plan far outweigh the advantages.

Conduct an Interview
Pretend you are a reporter working for a large Florida newspaper in 1924. You have just interviewed a man who discovered that the land he purchased sight unseen is located on swampland 65 miles from the nearest city. Write a one-page newspaper article telling about his experience.

Chicago
March 16, 1930

Today I came home and cried. I came home to my snug, warm apartment and completely broke down.

Why am I so miserable? This afternoon, for the first time, I stood outside a soup kitchen and watched people lined up for a free meal. I watched their faces and their demeanor. I sensed their shame and their embarrassment at being reduced to such straits.

"Oh, I'm not here for a free meal," one woman assured me. "My friend Irma is helping to serve soup inside. I just thought I'd drop by and chat with her for awhile."

"No, I'm not looking for a handout," a shabbily dressed young man said. "I just want to go inside and warm up a bit."

It is apparent that many of these unfortunate people are going through a period of denial. Just a few months ago, they had homes and apartments and automobiles. Now they can't afford a decent meal. My heart goes out to them. I can imagine their embarrassment—and possibly even their feelings of guilt—as they queue up for their daily dole.

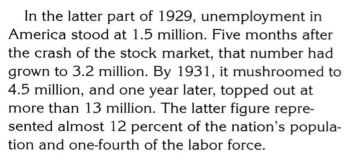

In the latter part of 1929, unemployment in America stood at 1.5 million. Five months after the crash of the stock market, that number had grown to 3.2 million. By 1931, it mushroomed to 4.5 million, and one year later, topped out at more than 13 million. The latter figure represented almost 12 percent of the nation's population and one-fourth of the labor force.

One result of such massive unemployment was the huge increase in bread lines and soup kitchens to feed the jobless. Soup kitchens operated out of missions, gymnasiums, and church basements. Even notorious gangster Al Capone established a soup kitchen in Chicago. The hungry and the unemployed could not be choosy about where they got a free meal. Often it was their only meal of the day.

Sometimes the needy waited in lines that extended for blocks just to get a doughnut and a hot cup of coffee. Afterward, the more destitute returned to the only home they knew: a cardboard box under a bridge or on the street. Even college students were not exempt from privation. Those on scholarships often had nothing to eat, while others were reduced to sleeping under bridges on campus.

Continued on page 11.

Continued from page 10.

Many men divided their days looking for work and scrounging for food. Some even resorted to retrieving scraps from garbage dumps. One literary critic in Chicago recalled seeing hundreds of people assembled at a dump awaiting the arrival of the garbage trucks. When the trucks dutifully arrived and dumped their contents in a heap, the hungry men literally dived into the mess and began searching for something edible. Neither the flies nor the stench deterred them from their mission.

No one knows how many Americans spurned the struggle for life in the cities and took to the road. Estimates run as high as two million. And perhaps as many as 200,000 were boys and girls. Hopping railroad freight cars, they roamed the country, looking for any kind of work they could find. At first, railroad employees threw them bodily from the trains, girls included. In 1932 alone, more than 683,000 train-jumpers were thrown from Southern Pacific boxcars. Finally, the railroads realized they were fighting a losing battle and began adding empty cars to accommodate the increasing number of drifters.

Those who rode the railroads fared little better than their city counterparts. Roaming from town to town, they ate at city missions and begged at back doors. Sometimes, in desperation, they stole to satisfy their hunger.

They were often beaten and thrown into jail. Sometimes they were abused or assaulted.

The 1930s were like no other time in the history of our nation. They were years that truly taxed the character and the resolve of the American people. Few were ever the same when the terrible period finally ended.

Discuss...

• how you would have felt having to accept a free meal at a soup kitchen.

• what effect the depression may have had on children and young people.

• what circumstances might have led some boys and girls to join the millions of hoboes who traveled the country on trains.

For Debate

Resolved: That it is the responsibility of the government to take care of its citizens during economic hard times.

New York City
December 11, 1930

Dear Tom,

Well, Christmas is coming on fast, and I just hope I can scrape together enough money to buy a few things for Rose and the baby. As you know, it's been a tough year. I'm just happy for you that you're in the army. At least you're eating well, and you have a roof over your head.

I'm managing to get by. Since I was laid off five weeks ago, I've been doing what a lot of fellows in New York are doing these days: selling apples on street corners. Sounds crazy, doesn't it? But it is work. It beats accepting handouts at the soup kitchen. Usually, I earn enough to buy a little something for Rose and me and the baby to eat for dinner. Not much, but it quiets the stomach rumbles for a few hours.

It's funny. It's not just guys like me out here selling apples. There are older men in fancy suits—former bigwigs in business, I suppose—standing on corners trying to earn a nickel too. These times are proving to be a great social leveler.

How are things at good old Fort Dix? Are you going home to Louisville for the holidays? If so, say hello to all the gang for me. Take care.

Your buddy,
Norman

In the fall of 1930, the International Apple Growers' Association, in an attempt to boost sagging sales, began to sell boxes of apples on credit to the jobless to peddle on the nation's streets. An energetic person who worked 12 long hours and sold his or her entire box might make a handsome profit of as much as $1.70!

Men and women would line up before dawn outside the office of the Apple Growers' Association to get their box. Each box contained 72 apples, and each apple sold for 5 cents. Before actually "opening for business," a peddler might pay 10 cents for paper bags to put the apples in and another 10 cents for subway fare. At the end of the day, if none of the apples were damaged and all were sold, the peddler would have taken in $3.60. After paying the association $1.75 for the box, and making allowance for the paper bags and the subway fare, the weary seller could pocket a profit of $1.70. If several apples were damaged and therefore unsalable, the amount of profit was usually lower.

Apple peddlers appeared on streets throughout America that dismal autumn of 1930. New York City alone had over 6,000 at one time. Along with bread lines and soup kitchens, they came to symbolize the hard times of the depression.

Discuss...

- why people would choose to sell apples on the street when they could get a free meal at a soup kitchen.

- what services are available to the unemployed today that did not exist during the Great Depression.

Create a Dialogue

Write a one-page paper reflecting the conversation between two children upon first observing their father selling apples on the street corner.

July 10, 1931

I am so hungry that I often sit for fear of fainting. But I must wait until tomorrow, when it is my turn to eat. Today, my little sister Claire gets whatever Daddy is able to bring home. Sometimes it's a few scraps from one of the soup kitchens; at other times it's something Daddy retrieved from the dump or from a garbage can at the back of a restaurant.

Our shack is one of many near the garbage dump. Daddy managed to scrounge together enough wood and tin to put it together. I helped as best I could. Our door and window are made of sacks, as is our floor. We have no stove. What will happen to us when winter comes?

I take comfort in my diary; it is my friend and constant companion. I am 14 years old, and I can't believe my world has turned completely upside down. Just a few months ago, I had a nice room in a comfortable little house. Daddy had a good job and Mama was still alive. Why is all of this happening?

Other symbols of the depression were shantytowns called "Hoovervilles." Named after President Herbert Hoover, who many thought did not fully grasp the seriousness of the economic situation, Hoovervilles sprang up near the downtown areas of large cities. They appeared in vacant lots, around garbage dumps, and in city parks. New York's famed Central Park even housed a Hooverville in the early 1930s. Hooverville shacks were built from every imaginable material: cardboard, tin, tarpaper, wood scraps, old signs, and fence posts. Sometimes, automobile parts were used in their construction. Photographs from the period show tin roofs held down by stones and other materials.

Deplorable as they were, Hooverville shanties were preferable to living in the open as many did.

Homeless persons could be found sleeping on sidewalks, under bridges, and on park benches. Those reduced to spending their nights on benches sought warmth under a "Hoover blanket," the depression term for a newspaper.

The poor who had a few pennies in their pockets might spend a night in a lodging facility run by a mission, the Salvation Army, or some other organization. For 10 or 15 cents, they could purchase the privilege of sleeping on a dirty blanket or mattress on a crowded floor. Some of these facilities were little more than flophouses infested with lice and rats.

Hoovervilles and the like were testimony to the worst years of the depression: 1929 to 1932. After 1932, with the election of Franklin Roosevelt, conditions slowly began to improve.

Discuss...

- how being jobless and homeless might affect a person's mental state.
- what agencies and charitable organizations offer assistance today to the poor and homeless.

Write a Letter

Pretend you are a student living in the early 1930s. Write a letter to President Hoover demanding that the government do more to help the homeless.

Journal Entry
December 29, 1932

It's not easy being a sheriff these days. Sometimes you must do your duty even when that duty goes against your conscience. That's what happened yesterday when a group of farmers tried to prevent the foreclosure of Fritz Kapp's dairy farm.

Old Fritz, like so many farmers in the country, had fallen behind on his payments to the bank and was scheduled to be evicted. Just as the papers were about to be served, some 75 farmers showed up on Fritz's behalf and tried to prevent his eviction. Heated words were exchanged and I thought, for a few moments, that a nasty fight was going to break out. My deputies, however, kept their heads and talked the group into leaving after 30 minutes.

I have mixed feelings about the farmers in this state. It breaks my heart to see so many of them literally being kicked off their lands. But it angers me to see the more radical of the farmers destroy their crops or dump their milk on the ground to try to force up prices. It's hard to believe this occurs when I read about kids in Appalachia so hungry that they are chewing on their own hands!

No industry suffered more during the depression than agriculture. Agriculture, in fact, had been on the decline since the end of World War I. Its problems only magnified when the bottom fell out of the economy in 1929.

Unlike other industries, agriculture did not share in the economic boom of the 1920s. While many Americans were enjoying the good life, farmers were suffering from high costs and low prices and, in many cases, the loss of their farms. Many struggled just to put food on the table.

The farmers' dilemma sprang from a decreased demand for farm products following World War I. During the war, farmers had been encouraged by the government to grow more food. Food was needed to fight the war and to supply America's allies. Thousands of farmers complied by borrowing money to buy more land and machinery. When the war ended and demand fell off sharply, there was a huge surplus of wheat, cotton, and other products. Farm prices fell accordingly, and farmers were unable to make the payments for the land and machinery they had purchased. Foreclosures on farms increased dramatically, and more and more farmers lost their means of livelihood. Some became tenants on land they had previously owned.

While most farmers during the depression coped as best they could within the law, a small percentage expressed their bitterness through acts of violence. Most of the violence occurred in Iowa, Wisconsin, and Minnesota, where angry farmers stopped trucks bound for market and destroyed their loads of fruit, vegetables, and eggs. They also dumped untold gallons of milk into ditches.

Farming conditions remained depressed until the Agricultural Adjustment Act of 1933, reduced surpluses by paying farmers a subsidy to limit production.

Discuss...

- to what extent the federal government was responsible for the farmers' plight during the 1930s.
- whether farmers were justified in destroying their produce to keep it off the market.
- the relationship between supply and demand and prices.

August 1, 1932

Dear Thelma,

My Timmy is dead. The army killed him, and he was only 11 weeks old. Who could have imagined that American soldiers would turn against their own people?

I wanted to leave Washington in June when most of the veterans and their families left. I wanted to go home to Oregon as fast as these two legs could carry me. But Billy wanted to stay. What choice did I have? Now my baby is dead because of it.

I'm sure you have read what happened last week at Anacostia Flats. The army came in and burned us out. Billy, the kids, and I ran inside a house on a road near the river. When the soldiers came by, one threw a tear-gas bomb near the door. Almost immediately our eyes began to burn, and Timmy started to vomit. I ran outside with him, where he continued to vomit. When he started to turn blue, we took him to the hospital. He died the next morning.

You're lucky you stayed in Oregon. I wish we had. We're in Johnstown, Pennsylvania, but we hope to be on the road home in a few days. Maybe I'll see you in a couple of weeks. Until then, pray for us.

Lottie

Farmers were not the only Americans calling the government's attention to their problems in the early 1930s. In the summer of 1932, thousands of veterans of World War I marched on Washington, D.C., demanding early payment on bonuses they were due to receive in 1945. Their march resulted in a clash with police and army troops that discredited the Hoover administration and helped elect Franklin Roosevelt a few months later.

The march of the Bonus Expeditionary Force, as the veterans called themselves, began innocently enough in May. Almost 20,000 veterans and their families from around the country descended on the nation's capital. They came by train, by truck, by car, and even on foot. They came asking Congress to grant their $1,000 bonuses 13 years early. They were hungry and jobless and insisted they needed the money to feed their families.

Most of the veterans took up residence in hastily constructed shantytowns that sprang up almost overnight. The largest of these was on land directly across the Anacostia River from the Capitol. It was here that most of the 20,000 demonstrators camped out during their stay in Washington.

The veterans waited patiently until the middle of June, when Congress deliberated on whether to honor their request. The House of Representatives voted to give the veterans their bonuses early, but the Senate rejected the proposal. Angry and disappointed, the vast majority of veterans nonetheless accepted Congress' decision and packed up and left the capital. Some 2,000

Continued on page 16.

Continued from page 15.

hardliners stayed, however, and it was this group that shortly came into conflict with the authorities.

The showdown came on the morning of July 28. It began when workmen came to tear down an abandoned government building that had provided shelter for some of the veterans. A fight ensued, and the police were called in. Soon veterans were hurling rocks and bricks, and a number of police officers were injured, including the chief of police. The battle raged throughout the day, prompting President Hoover at 3:00 P.M. to call a detachment of cavalry from nearby Fort Myer. Placed under the command of General Douglas MacArthur,

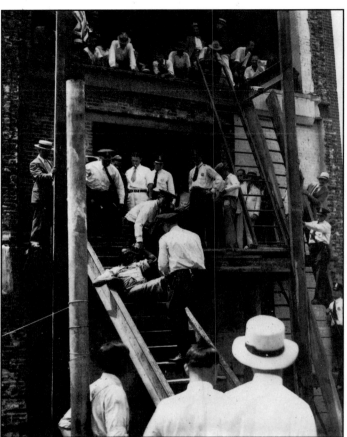

the army's chief of staff, soldiers armed with guns and tanks soon confronted the veterans. Firearms, sabers, and tear gas were unleashed against the demonstrators. The soldiers marched to the Hooverville established at Anacostia Flats and set fire to all of the shanties. In the course of the action, several people were killed, including an 11-week-old baby. Scores of people were injured, some of them women and children.

By the following morning, the battered veterans began to retreat into Maryland and Pennsylvania. The "revolution," as some Americans, including General MacArthur, viewed it, had been put down. Its climax marked an inglorious end to the White House term of Herbert Hoover.

Discuss...

- whether the government acted correctly in denying World War I veterans their bonuses early.
- how the individual soldier must feel when forced to carry out an unpopular order.
- if violence is ever justified as a means to gain an end.

For Debate

Resolved: That the United States Army was justified in using force against the veterans at Anacostia Flats.

Resolved: That persons who serve in the armed forces are entitled to special privileges.

Wheeling, West Virginia
November 1932

Well, we just heard the news on the radio. Mr. Roosevelt got himself elected, and Mama and Papa are dancing a jig in the kitchen. Papa has nearly worked himself to death in the mine for less than $3 a day. He says that Mr. Roosevelt is going to do something about it. I hope so.

I'm only 11 years old, and I have to admit that I don't understand a lot about what's been going on. But I've heard Mama and Papa talk about Mr. Roosevelt's New Deal, and it sounds good to me. I'm in favor of anything that might give me something to eat other than dandelions and blackberries.

As 1932 neared an end and a new presidential election approached, the Great Depression in America worsened. Almost 14 million workers were unemployed, and hundreds of banks were closed. Many factories had shut down and more than 85,000 small businesses had gone bankrupt. Bread lines and Hoovervilles haunted every major city. Farmers were destroying their crops and patrolling their lands with shotguns to prevent foreclosures. The nation was on the brink of economic disaster.

While the Bonus Army was still encamped in the nation's capital, the Democratic Party held its convention in Chicago. Amid high hopes and great fanfare, they nominated New York Governor Franklin Delano Roosevelt as their candidate. The Republicans tabbed President Hoover to once again carry their party's banner.

The election in November was not even close. Roosevelt won a landslide victory with 472 electoral votes to Hoover's 59. He carried all but six states and received almost 23 million popular votes to Hoover's 16 million. The New York governor was given a mandate from the American people to do something about the depression.

Twenty-three million voters put their faith in Roosevelt's New Deal, through which the Democratic challenger had vowed to enact programs to end the Great Depression. After winning the election and upon being inaugurated on March 4th (the last chief executive to take office on that date), the new president was expected to make good on his promises.

Discuss...

- why millions of citizens still cast their votes with Hoover.
- what might have happened if President Hoover had been reelected in 1932.
- why you think the inauguration date of U.S. presidents was moved from March 4th to January 20th.
- why the Great Depression that began in the United States quickly spread to Europe.

For Further Study

Franklin Roosevelt was elected by a wide margin over Herbert Hoover in 1932. But other presidents have enjoyed victories just as impressive. Compare Roosevelt's electoral votes in 1932 with those garnered by Lyndon Johnson in 1964 and Ronald Reagan in 1980.

Washington, D.C.
May 12, 1933

Today, we gave the president his Federal Emergency Relief Act. On March 21, we gave our approval to the Civilian Conservation Corps. Five days before that, on March 16, we passed the Agricultural Adjustment Act. Everything the president asks for we are giving him.

Are we moving too fast? Only time will tell. Right now, the president has the unanimous support of both houses of Congress. There are, to be sure, dissenters. Some maintain that the president is asking for too much power and that the New Deal smacks of socialism. Others, myself included, wonder how in the world we are going to pay for all of this.

But at least we're moving ahead. At least something is finally being done to help this nation and its millions of wretched citizens. I salute the president for his direction and his resolve.

The first 99 days of Franklin Roosevelt's presidency are called the Hundred Days. During that time, a special session of Congress granted the new president emergency powers to cope with the nation's economic problems. From March 9 to June 16, Roosevelt proposed more legislative acts than had any president before him, all of which were approved by both the House and the Senate.

But even before Congress convened, the president had swung into action. On the day of his inauguration, Roosevelt ordered all banks closed for four days to give Congress time to come up with a plan to stabilize the ailing institutions. Banks that proved to be stable were shored up with federal money and allowed to reopen. As a further measure, a new agency, the Federal Deposit Insurance Corporation, was established to insure depositors' savings accounts. Ever so slowly, the public's trust in banks was restored.

Roosevelt tackled other problems just as swiftly. An agricultural law provided subsidies to farmers to limit acreage, a move aimed at eliminating surpluses and raising farm prices. A public works program was started that gave employment to millions on such projects as roads, dams, parks, and playgrounds. An emergency relief program channeled funds to state and local agencies to provide financial assistance to the unemployed. Finally, what was called the Civilian Conservation Corps gave outdoor employment to thousands of young men between the ages of 17 and 33. Because of its popularity at the time and its interest to young readers today, the Civilian Conservation Corps is discussed in more detail in the next unit.

Discuss...

- whether the New Deal programs of President Roosevelt were socialistic in nature.

- why Congress, which is often at odds with the White House, would approve all of President Roosevelt's proposals during the Hundred Days.

- which programs started by Franklin Roosevelt are in effect today.

For Further Study

The numerous government agencies established during the New Deal era are often called the "alphabet agencies." Some are discussed in this book, some are not. Research those listed below. Write the full name of each and a sentence explaining its functions: AAA, PWA, CWA, TVA, SEC, FERA.

Near Missoula, Montana
February 5, 1934

Dear Hank,

I wish you had enlisted and come with me. For the first time in five years, I find myself laughing again and looking to the future with hope. Sure—the work is hard and the hours are long. The living accommodations can't compete with the Biltmore, but at least we're indoors and warm. And the food, though not exactly of the gourmet variety, is healthful and plentiful. In two months, I've put on more than 15 pounds.

We came out here part of the way by train, and then transferred to some dilapidated trucks for the final leg of the trip. After we had bounced for what seemed an eternity over the worst road ever built, we finally arrived at what we perceived to be our destination. But upon dismounting from the trucks, we saw no buildings. Nothing. Nothing but trees—everywhere you looked.

"Hey Sarge!" shouted one of my buddies. "Where's the camp?"

"You're standing right in the middle of it, son," answered Sergeant Watson. "And if you don't want to spend too many nights sleeping on the cold ground, you'd best grab some axes and start chopping!"

Well, to make a long story short, we did chop. And we chopped and chopped some more. And you know what? We built that camp from scratch: the cabins, the mess hall, the whole thing. We built it ourselves. And I think I can say that every one of us was proud. It was quite a feeling of accomplishment.

Well, Hank, take care, and drop me a line. Think about joining up! It beats working for pennies in the day and trying to go to college at night. Think about it.

Your buddy,
Eliot

The Civilian Conservation Corps (CCC) was the first of President Roosevelt's New Deal programs to go into action. It was also the most popular. Roosevelt himself conceived the idea of the corps in March 1933. He saw it as a way to conserve the nation's natural resources and at the same time take idle, young men off the streets and offer them gainful employment. The program was a success from the start. Even opponents of the New Deal spoke approvingly of the CCC.

The CCC was similar to a volunteer army.

Young men enlisted in cities throughout America and then were sent to camps throughout the country. Most of these camps were located in parks and national forests, and some, as the letter above indicates, were built by the recruits themselves. Originally, there were 1,468 camps, a number that grew to 2,650 in two years. The corps began with 250,000 enrollees in 1933 and ballooned to a total number of 3 million by 1942, the year it was disbanded. Members were paid $30 a month, $25 of which was sent to their families back home. If a young man's family was

Continued on page 20.

Continued from page 19.

not on relief (most were) and was not in need of help, the $25 was deposited each month in a special account and given to him when his enlistment was up.

Under the supervision of military personnel and park rangers, the men of the Civilian Conservation Corps performed a wide variety of labor. They cleared out dead and diseased trees and planted more than 1.3 billion new ones. They built campgrounds, bridges, dams, roads, and recreational facilities. They fought forest fires, constructed firebreaks, and strung miles of telephone lines. They even conducted wildlife surveys, stocked streams with fish, and set up bird sanctuaries. All told, corps members worked at more than 300 different kinds of jobs.

Enrollment in the CCC influenced members for life. In the beginning, most were bitter, undisciplined, and undernourished youth. They had no work experience and little hope for the future. In just a few short months, both their appearance and their demeanor changed. Fresh air, wholesome food, hard work, and good friendships transformed them into robust, young men. Because of experience gained in the camps, many were better able to find jobs when their nine-month enrollment ended.

Employers, in fact, often gave preference to former CCC members because of the discipline and work ethic they had acquired.

The men of the CCC also bettered themselves educationally. Over 100,000 learned to read and write, while 25,000 received eighth-grade certificates and 5,000 earned high-school diplomas. Others were able to take college courses offered in the camps.

Again, the Civilian Conservation Corps was one of the most successful programs of the New Deal. The role it played at a critical time in American history cannot be overestimated.

Discuss...

• why comradeship and a sense of belonging are important to the well-being of an individual.

• how life in the Civilian Conservation Corps was similar to that in the military.

• whether you—if you had been a young man living during the Great Depression—would have enlisted in the CCC.

"Chickens Gun Down the Blue Eagle!"

NEWS SPECIAL
Washington, D.C.
May 28, 1935

Don't ever sell chickens short. Yesterday, they sent President Roosevelt's blue eagle plummeting from the sky in a ball of flames. The eagle's demise is certain to be cheered by countless businesses throughout the country.

By unanimous decision, the Supreme Court has dealt the death blow to the National Recovery Administration. In the case of the Schechter Poultry Corporation vs. the United States, the court ruled that the NRA is unconstitutional because it grants legislative powers to the president. Its decision is a severe blow to the president and his New Deal.

The case came to the Court when the NRA accused the Schechter Poultry Corporation of selling diseased chickens. In addition, the NRA charged that the small Brooklyn firm had not paid the minimum wage established by the fair practices code. The Schechters shot back that since they were not engaged in interstate commerce, it was none of the NRA's business what they were doing or how much they paid their employees. Furthermore, they asserted all along that the NRA was unconstitutional. So the Schechters took the federal boys to court. When the case reached the hallowed halls of the Supreme Court, the nine robed gentlemen sitting therein agreed with the Schechters, and the NRA was as good as dead.

When it was enacted on June 16, 1933, President Roosevelt considered the National Industrial Recovery Act his most important New Deal legislation. He hoped it would stimulate the economy and put people back to work. For a while, it succeeded in doing both.

The National Industrial Recovery Act consisted of two parts. The first established the Public Works Administration and was designed to put the unemployed to work on publicly funded projects. The second set up the National Recovery Administration (NRA). The National Recovery Administration encouraged businesses and industries to adhere to a set of codes or rules regulating wages, hours, production, and prices. Those who joined and promised to comply with the codes either flew a flag or displayed a poster of the NRA's blue eagle emblem, under which was inscribed the organization's motto: "We Do Our Part."

The Public Works Administration financed more than 34,000 programs throughout the country. It built dams, highways, schools, hospitals, and housing projects. But the PWA employed mostly skilled labor and did not address the needs of millions of unskilled workers. It was replaced in 1935 by the Works Progress Administration (name changed to Works Projects Administration in 1939), which provided employment for lesser-skilled Americans. Although some of the projects financed by the WPA were of little value, some, such as parks and playgrounds, proved beneficial to the nation.

Continued on page 22.

Continued from page 21.

The National Recovery Administration had trouble from the start. Many businesses refused to join, and others found ways to circumvent the codes. Smaller businesses charged that the rules set forth gave an advantage to larger firms. However, the NRA did put into motion legislation that greatly improved the lot of workers. Before it was axed by the Supreme Court as unconstitutional in 1935, the NRA abolished child labor, set a minimum wage of 30 cents an hour, and put many of the nation's sweatshops out of business.

Two other provisions of the NRA concerning labor-management relations appeared in later bills. The Wagner Act of 1935, also called the National Labor Relations Act, strengthened labor unions and gave workers the right of collective bargaining. This meant that employers had to sit down with workers' representatives and discuss wages, hours, and working conditions. For many years, individual workers who petitioned their employers for increased wages or better working conditions could be fired without any hope of redress.

A second law that grew out of the NRA was the Fair Labor Standards Act of 1938. It increased the minimum wage to 40 cents an hour and required that employers pay time-and-a-half for work weeks exceeding 44 hours. The act also forbade the hiring of children under the age of 16.

Discuss...

- how collective bargaining protects the individual worker.
- why children under the age of 16 are not permitted to have full-time jobs.
- whether employers should be free to set their own wage scales and working conditions.

For Debate

Resolved: That it is the responsibility of the federal government to regulate business and industry for the good of the people.

Write a Letter

Write a letter to your congressman or congresswoman insisting that the present minimum wage be increased. Give reasons justifying such an increase.

September 10, 1934

Tonight we're camped with several other families just west of Flagstaff, Arizona. It's our third day on the road, and it's been the worst. The baby is sick and crying all the time. The twins have been nothing but trouble. Lloyd says we should cross the California line by tomorrow afternoon. I hope so. I hope the old jalopy holds together one more day.

We left Oklahoma with just enough money for gas and food, and precious little food at that. Other than a couple of old mattresses and bedsprings and pots and pans stacked on the car, that's all we have. Even this journal I'm keeping is now being written on old paper bags.

We had no choice but to leave. It hadn't rained in 18 months. When all the crops died, the winds started blowing the soil away. There were days when the sky was as dark as night from the black dust. The house and the barn were half buried in sand most of the time. If you went out, you had to cover your face with a handkerchief to keep the dirt out of your eyes and your mouth. Even then, when you came back inside, your mouth was full of the stuff. And the cow! If I live forever, I will never forget her pitiful cries from the barn for water. It was a relief when the poor thing finally died.

They say there's plenty of work in California. Well, we'll find out soon enough, I suppose. Anything has to be better than what we left behind.

By 1934, the worst part of the Great Depression was over, and the nation had started on the slow road to recovery. But there was one section of the country where the programs of the New Deal had had little or no effect on economic conditions. That area was a part of the Great Plains that came to be called the Dust Bowl.

You will recall that farmers during World War I had been encouraged to produce surpluses to meet the needs of wartime. Farmers on the Great Plains, like those everywhere, overplanted their fields to take advantage of this increased demand. But whereas surpluses resulted in falling prices and bank foreclosures in most parts of the country, the farmers of the Plains had to cope with an added problem: they saw winds literally blow their farms away.

For many years, the Great Plains had been overgrazed and overfarmed. Livestock were allowed to slowly destroy the precious vegetation necessary to hold the soil in place, and farmers employed unwise farming methods in their drive to increase production. Land was never allowed to lie fallow to maintain its fertility, and careless plowing left fields open to erosion. Added to this was the scarcity of rain. Average annual rainfall on the Plains is from 10 to 20 inches, compared to 40 or more in other farming regions. When rain did come in the 1930s, it often came in torrents, washing away the abused soil. When there was little or no rain, as was often the case, winds simply picked up the topsoil and blew it away. As much as 300 million tons of topsoil could be carried away in a two-day storm. (Farmers on the Plains quipped that they could stand by their windows and count their neighbors' farms as they blew past.) Dust from the Plains, carried by the jet stream, darkened skies all the way to the East Coast. It was so bad that streetlights in such eastern cities as New York and Boston often burned during the middle of the day.

Continued on page 24.

Continued from page 23.

From 1933 to 1936, dust storms ravaged parts of Kansas, Nebraska, New Mexico, Colorado, Texas, and Oklahoma. It is not surprising that thousands of farmers gave up and moved west to California, hoping to find a better life. Because so many of those who jammed the highways out of the Dust Bowl were from Oklahoma, the name "Okies" came to be applied to all of them.

Few Okies found the good life in California. Most became migrant workers laboring for

pennies a day in the fields and living in shacks and shanties that often sprang up near dirty irrigation ditches. Since water from these ditches was used for cooking, serious health problems soon arose. Children of migrant workers suffered from cramps, diarrhea, dysentery, pellagra, hookworm, and rickets. Many died.

From 1933 to 1936, more than 300,000 farm families migrated to California. Competition for work was keen. When a grower advertised for help, sometimes three times as many pickers showed up than were needed. Such an excess of labor allowed growers to pay desperate migrants as little as 45 cents on some days.

Low wages and sordid living conditions were the plight of migrant workers through the Great Depression years. Their tragic story is described by John Steinbeck in his Pulitizer prize-winning novel, *The Grapes of Wrath.*

Discuss...

- what conservation practices might have prevented the Dust Bowl.
- why migrant workers are sometimes the subject of scorn and even abuse by others.

Create a Dialogue

Create a dialogue between an Oklahoma farmer and his wife contemplating abandoning their farm in the 1930s and moving to California.

For Further Study

Look up hookworm, dysentery, pellegra, and rickets in an encyclopedia. List their causes and symptoms, and explain how they can be prevented and/or cured.

August 17, 1935

I was pleased to hear that Congress passed the Social Security Act a few days ago. It was long overdue. As a history teacher, I am aware that Germany enacted old-age insurance as early as 1899. Other European nations followed suit as time went on. Finally, the United States is catching up with the rest of the world.

Although some states have looked after their poor and needy for some time, the Social Security Act represents the first legislation of its kind passed at the national level. One of the law's main provisions is to provide a monthly pension for people over the age of 65. Beginning in 1940, most retirees over that age will receive a check each month from the federal government. The amount of the check will not be enough to cover every need, but it should suffice to keep food on the table and a roof over the head.

The new law relieves two concerns of mine. Not only can I stop worrying about what I will do when I am too old to work, but I can also take comfort in knowing that I will not become a financial burden to my children or to others. Such worries must have haunted people in the past.

Another highlight of Franklin Roosevelt's first administration was the passage of the Social Security Act in August 1935. Although America had always had its unemployed and needy, their numbers were never so great as during the depression years. The Social Security Act was passed at a most opportune time.

The Social Security Act contained several programs. One program provided public assistance to the needy and to those who were already too old to work. Another provided for child welfare. By far the largest program dealt with social insurance. It allowed for payments for unemployment, workmen's compensation, disabilities, and retirement. Regarding the latter, a designated percentage was deducted from each worker's paycheck for future Social Security benefits. His or her employer matched the amount, and the money was sent to Washington to be held until the beneficiary retired. Since 1935, the amount deducted from paychecks has increased proportionally to the amount earned by the worker. The benefit a person receives upon retirement depends on how many years he or she has worked and how much money he or she has paid into the system in Social Security taxes.

One part of the original Social Security bill was deleted before Congress approved the act in 1935. That part consisted of a plan for national health insurance. It was removed because of intense pressure from the American Medical Association, who saw it as a form of socialized medicine. National health insurance remains a major issue today.

Discuss...

- whether workers should have a choice of not participating in the Social Security program.
- whether private charities and local agencies, and not the federal government, could better address the needs of welfare recipients.
- what other sources of income retired persons should plan on to supplement their Social Security benefits.

For Debate

Resolved: That the health and medical needs of the American people can best be served through a system of national health insurance.

November 1, 1938

Dear Laura,

Did you hear that crazy program on the Mercury Theatre of the Air the other night—the one that created such an uproar? Of course you did; you always listen to that. And I bet you almost had a heart attack just like Irvin and I.

Like a lot of people, we tuned in late and took the Martian invasion for real. What with all the screaming and explosions, who could have guessed it was only an adaptation of "War of the Worlds"? Why, it almost scared Irvin and me to death. My mind conjured up images of being assaulted by little green men and even being whisked away to Mars in a spaceship. Irvin went so far as to load the 12-gauge.

When it was over, it was all kind of funny. At the height of the "invasion," Sid and Mabel next door threw a few things in their car and headed east to Pensacola. Why they thought Pensacola might be safer than Mobile is beyond me.

Write and tell me what you and Papa thought about the whole thing. I'm sure Papa didn't take it seriously for one minute. Bye now, and wri

Love,
Katie

In spite of their problems, Americans during the depression years kept themselves entertained. Some 27 million households had radios, and listening to it constituted the main leisure activity for some families. They relied on the radio for news, weather forecasts, and sports and eagerly looked forward to President Roosevelt's frequent "fireside chats" via the air waves. Sometimes, dramas like the one discussed in the letter above both thrilled and frightened them.

Going to the movies was also popular. For a mere dime, a person could go to one of the more than 15,000 theaters in America and enjoy a double feature. Films of the day were generally lighthearted and usually avoided topics that reminded people of their everyday concerns. Sixty percent of Americans went to the movies once a week.

Jigsaw puzzles first appeared during the Great Depression and became an immediate craze. First constructed of plywood and therefore expensive, they were soon being made of cardboard and priced within the range of almost everyone. Puzzles took peoples' minds off their problems and gave them a sense of accomplishment. Jigsaw clubs, where buffs exchanged puzzles, sprang up everywhere.

Some forms of entertainment were carry-overs from the 1920s. Dance marathons, flagpole sitting, and other stunts provided diversions from the cares of everyday life.

Discuss...

• how forms of entertainment have changed since the 1930s.

• whether you think young people were bored with the kinds of entertainment available to them during the Great Depression.

• why the subject matter of films (and radio and television programs) today is so vastly different from that of the 1930s.

• whether you agree with regulations that restrict what can be shown on television and in films.

NEWS BULLETIN
Chicago, Illinois
July 22, 1934

John Herbert Dillinger, just last month named Public Enemy Number 1 by the FBI, was gunned down at 10:30 tonight by federal agents outside this city's Biograph Theater. Thus ends the brief career of a vicious desperado who, in 13 short months, terrorized the Midwest and who was responsible, either directly or indirectly, for the deaths of some 20 law enforcement officers and several innocent bestanders.

The economic hard times of the 1930s did more than cause mass unemployment and create bread lines. They also brought about a brief crime wave engineered by a different kind of gangster: the bank robber.

Prior to 1933, gangsterism in America was primarily associated with bootlegging, which is the transport and sale of illegal alcohol. But when the 21st Amendment repealed prohibition and made alcohol legal again, some criminals switched their activities to robbing banks. And ludicrous as it may seem, they had the unproclaimed support of countless Americans. Many people saw banks as villains that fore-closed on farms and homes and threw desperate people into the streets. So when a bank robber such as John Dillinger or Baby-Face Nelson or Machine-Gun Kelly robbed a bank, there were actually people who cheered their efforts. Some Americans no doubt envied these desperados of the Great Depression who had overcome hard times by getting something for nothing.

John Dillinger and other desperados robbed countless banks across the Midwest in 1933 and 1934. That these bloodthirsty killers had become folk heroes to some is borne out by the behavior of Chicagoans when Dillinger was shot on a hot July night in 1934. A car parked near the scene of the shootout was dismantled by souvenir seekers who thought it belonged to Dillinger. A number of people, once Dillinger's body was removed to the morgue, dipped their handker-chiefs or pieces of paper in the blood left on the sidewalk. Women were even observed dipping the hems of their skirts in the small pool left behind. But there is more. Melvin Purvis, the FBI agent who cornered Dillinger as he came out of a Chicago theater, was offered $50 by a souvenir hunter because his white pants were spotted red. And then there was the person who offered Dillinger's father $10,000 for the body!

Because of stepped-up efforts by the FBI, the era of the bank outlaw was brief. Most of those who had chosen to follow the path were killed or captured long before the depression ended.

Discuss...

- why you think some people are fascinated by criminals and their activities.
- whether the 21st Amendment, which ended the Prohibition era, was good or bad for the country.

Conduct a Survey

Ask five people what steps they think the government should take to bring crime and violence under control in America. Report your findings to the class.

July 19, 1935

I don't know why I went. Perhaps it was out of curiosity, or maybe it was because Billy kept telling me I would see something I'd never forget. He was right on that score. If I live to be a hundred, I will never be able to erase from my mind the scene at that tree.

What happened is difficult to comprehend. Billy said a white woman accused Rubin Stacy of "threatening and frightening her." Not waiting for an arrest and a possible trial, a group of hotheads seized Rubin and dragged him screaming out of town. After a crowd had gathered at a pre-announced place, the hotheads lynched the poor fellow from an oak tree. I thought his struggling body would never go limp.

I was horrified at the reaction of the mob that had come to see "justice done." Some of the white men had smiles and smirks on their faces as they commented that Rubin Stacy had gotten what he deserved. They joked and teased and treated the whole thing like some kind of amusement. The few blacks there stood in deathly silence. I don't know what they were thinking.

Among the crowd were a number of small children. I recognized Bertha Stedman's five- and six-year-old daughters. Bertha herself had a camera, taking pictures of the dangling body.

I ran behind the nearest clump of bushes and vomited.

No one suffered more during the Great Depression than black Americans. Always the "last hired and the first fired," their unemployment rate was much higher than that of whites. In some cities, blacks constituted over 70 percent of the total number of unemployed.

To be sure, black Americans benefited from the New Deal. Many worked on government projects and were paid well for their labor. Share-croppers and farm laborers also received help from the Roosevelt Administration. There were even black divisions of the Civilian Conservation Corps, although most were under the command of white officers.

While President Roosevelt often invited black leaders to the White House and placed a number of them in government offices, there was a blight against his record that many black Americans would never forget. That was his reluctance to fully support a federal antilynch law.

Continued on page 29.

Continued from page 28.

Lynching was not new to America. Mobs had hanged horse thieves and robbers since colonial times. But until about 1890, most lynch victims were white. After that date, the victims were usually black. Most lynchings occurred in the South, although they took place in all sections of the country except New England. The peak year for lynchings during the depression was 1935, when a lynching occurred at the rate of one every three weeks.

Antilynch legislation was first introduced in the Congress in 1899. Defeated soundly, it was introduced again in 1919 and 1922. In 1922, it passed the House but died in the Senate. It reappeared in 1934 at the height of Roosevelt's New Deal.

In 1934, there was strong support for an anti-lynch law, even in the South. "Enough is enough," was the sentiment expressed by Americans nationwide. But President Roosevelt hedged on his support of such legislation. His reason seemed purely political. Southerners chaired important committees in both the House and the Senate, and the president feared they would block other New Deal legislation if he pushed too hard on an antilynch law. So the law failed again, as it was destined to do also in 1935 and 1938.

Eventually, most states passed their own laws against lynching and the practice gradually stopped. But there were still a few that took place even into the 1960s.

Discuss...

- how ignorance and fear contribute to prejudice.
- whether prejudice is a regional or a nationwide problem.
- if complete racial equality and harmony are attainable.

Create a Dialogue

Imagine yourself a black American breadwinner of the 1930s who has just been laid off from your job. Create a dialogue between yourself and your spouse reflecting your feelings at the time, as well as your plans for the future.

Write a Letter

Pretend you are living in the 1930s. Write a letter to President Roosevelt urging him to support an antilynch law.

Popularity, Resistance, and Roosevelt's Second Term

Chicago Tribune
Editorial
February 10, 1937

The man is drunk with power. One would think the authority granted him through his New Deal legislation would be enough. But he obviously wants more. Now he is attempting to scrap the Constitution and pack the Supreme Court.

The president has asked Congress to change the structure of our nation's highest tribunal. He seeks the power to appoint one additional judge for every judge who is 70 years old but who has not retired. Since 6 of the 9 justices are over 70 years old, Mr. Roosevelt would increase the court's size to 15. His 6 new appointees, to be sure, would be liberal

in philosophy and supportive of his programs.

This columnist, as do many Americans, sincerely hopes that Congress will not give Mr. Roosevelt what he wants. To do so would make the Court the president's personal tool and seriously jeopardize our system of checks and balances.

The above editorial demonstrates that President Roosevelt, like all presidents, had his detractors. But after looking at the election results of 1936, one might think quite the opposite.

Roosevelt was so confident of being reelected in 1936 that he did not campaign seriously until October. His faith in his popularity was borne out at the polls. In a smashing victory, the incumbent president defeated Republican candidate Alfred Landon by an overwhelming majority. Roosevelt received 523 electoral votes to Landon's 8. The popular vote was equally as convincing, with the president getting 27,476,673 votes to Landon's 16,679,583. Landon carried just two states: Maine and Vermont. The huge margin of victory seemed to indicate that the average American was pleased with the results of Roosevelt's first term.

Roosevelt's second four years were characterized by arguments with Congress and the Supreme Court. Because the Court had declared several of his New Deal programs unconstitutional, the president sought to make it more liberal by increasing the number of justices from 9 to15. After a bitter fight in Congress, his "courtpacking" bill was defeated. Debate over the radical proposal caused a rift within the ranks of the Democratic Party.

After continuing on the upswing during Roosevelt's first term, the economy fluctuated considerably during his second. When he decided to balance the budget in 1937 by cutting spending, business and industry went into a tailspin. By March 1948, four million additional Americans joined the ranks of the unemployed. When the president reversed himself and increased spending again, the economy rebounded. Such ups and downs would continue until World War II brought a final end to the Great Depression.

Franklin Roosevelt was elected to a third term in 1940 and to a fourth in 1944. He died four months into his final term.

Discuss...

- whether changing the number of justices on the Supreme Court would make it more or less effective.
- whether President Roosevelt's attempt to "pack" the Supreme Court was an unconstitutional move.
- the reasons behind the 22nd Amendment in 1951, that limited the president of the United States to two terms.

U.S. Naval Air Station
Lakehurst, New Jersey
May 7, 1937

Dear Mom and Dad,

   I just wanted to write to let you know I'm okay. I was off duty and not at the mooring mast when the Hindenburg blew up last night. But I was close enough to see the flames and hear those unfortunate people screaming. Some of my buddies said a number of passengers ran from the flames with their clothes on fire and their faces badly burned. Somebody said they thought 36 people were killed. I'm not sure how many were on board when the airship left Europe.

   It's difficult to believe that something like this could happen after all those trips. I read the other day that the Hindenburg had crossed the Atlantic over 30 times without incident. For the thing to just blow up is inconceivable.

   I have to go. It's time for my duty. Take care—and write.

                                        Love,
                                        Johnny

The explosion of the *Hindenburg*, which ended the brief age of airship travel, was but one of many dramatic events that occurred in America and throughout the world in the 1930s. Some others are summarized below.

The year 1930 saw the end of silent movies, while 1931 was highlighted by the opening of the George Washington Bridge in New York. Thomas Edison died, and Japan invaded Manchuria in that year.

In 1932, the baby of famed aviator Charles Lindbergh was kidnapped and murdered, and Amelia Earhart became the first woman to fly solo over the Atlantic. Five years later, Ms. Earhart disappeared over the Pacific while attempting to fly around the world.

In 1933, Adolf Hitler came to power in Germany, prompting scientist Albert Einstein to emigrate to America one year later. In 1935, Italy invaded Ethiopia, and in the following year, a civil war broke out in Spain that ultimately led to the fascist dictatorship of Francisco Franco. Also in 1936, King Edward VIII of England shocked the world by giving up his throne to marry Baltimore divorcee Wallis Warfield Simpson.

In 1937, Japan invaded China, and the following year, Germany seized Austria and Czechoslovakia. Then, in 1939, Adolf Hitler attacked Poland, setting off the Second World War.

As mentioned earlier in this book, the beginning of World War II finally brought the depression to an end. But the people of the world had little time to relax and enjoy the renewed prosperity. They were faced with a terrible war that would drag on for six long years.

Discuss...

• how economic problems within countries make it possible for dictators to attain power.

• which worldwide event of the 1930s had the greatest impact on the world of the 1940s.

Write a Summary

Write a one-page summary of life in America during the years of the Great Depression.

A New President, a New Hope—page 17

Lyndon Johnson in 1964 had 486 electoral votes. Ronald Reagan in 1980 had 489.

The Hundred Days—page 18

1. PWA—Public Works Administration—set up long-term programs that provided jobs for the unemployed building dams, bridges, roads, etc.

2. CWA—Civil Works Administration—was established to provide more immediate employment on government projects.

3. TVA—Tennessee River Valley Authority—built dams, power plants, etc.

4. SEC—Securities and Exchange Commission—established to regulate stock market practices.

5. FERA—Federal Emergency Relief Administration—provided funds to states to help the needy.

Dust and Desperation—page 24

Hookworm—caused by a small roundworm that usually enters the body through the feet and invades the small intestine. Symptoms include weakness and anemia. Hookworms can be treated with drugs. Recovery is aided by a diet rich in proteins, vitamins, and iron.

Dysentery—may be caused by an amoeba or bacteria. It is characterized by diarrhea with blood and mucus. Dysentery responds well to drugs and can be prevented through cleanliness, sanitation, and purification of water and sewage.

Pellagra—caused by a lack of niacin and Vitamin-B complex. Symptoms include nervousness, fatigue, and inflammation of the skin. Can cause mental disorders if left untreated. Can be prevented by a diet that includes fresh lean beef, yeast, and other foods high in protein.

Rickets—caused by a lack of Vitamin D and calcium. Results in softening and bending of the bones. Is prevented by a proper diet that includes enough calcium and Vitamin D.

Selected Bibliography

Butterfield, Roger. *The American Past*. New York: Simon and Schuster, 1966.

Chandler, Lester V. *America's Greatest Depression, 1929–1941*. New York: Harper & Row, Publishers, 1970.

Galbraith, John Kenneth. *The Great Crash 1929*. Boston: Houghton Mifflin Company, 1972.

Harris, Nathaniel. *The Great Depression*. Living Through History series. London: B.T. Batsford Ltd., 1988.

Horan, James D. *The Desperate Years*. New York: Bonanza Books, 1962.

Leuchtenburg, William E., and the editors of Life. *New Deal and Global War*. New York: Time Incorporated, 1964.

Watkins, Tom H. *The Great Depression*. Boston: Little, Brown, and Company, 1993.